SACRAMENTO
RIVER

SAN LEANDRO

SAN FRANCISCO
BAY

HAYWARD

SAN MATEO
BRIDGE

FREMONT

SAN MATEO

DUMBARTON
BRIDGE

REDWOOD CITY

SAN JOSE

To Mikka and Maggie

Published by
Heian / Stone Bridge Press
P.O. Box 8208, Berkeley, CA 94707
tel 510-524-8732 · sbp@stonebridge.com · www.stonebridge.com

Story © Wendy Tokuda and Richard Hall
Illustrations © Hanako Wakiyama

First paperback edition, 1992
First revised edition, 2014

Printed in China.

p-ISBN: 978-1-61172-017-4
e-ISBN: 978-1-61172-511-7

Humphrey
The Lost Whale
A True Story

story by Wendy Tokuda and Richard Hall

illustrations by Hanako Wakiyama

HEIAN

Our story begins on a sunny day, far out at sea. A pod of humpback whales was traveling south together for the winter. Humpback whales are magnificent creatures that sing beautiful songs to each other underwater. In the whole world

there are very few of them, so each one is quite special.

And they are intelligent. Every winter they travel south, every summer they head north, and they always know the way.

But even whales can make mistakes. One whale named Humphrey made a big one. He turned away from his friends and wandered under the Golden Gate Bridge into San Francisco Bay.

Everyone was surprised to see Humphrey in the Bay! People don't get to see humpback whales very often because they usually stay in very deep waters. It was a special treat to see one so close to the city of San Francisco.

Humphrey was a spectacular sight—as long as a city bus and as big as seven elephants put together. He would come up to breathe, appearing as if by magic, and people would stop whatever they were doing to watch him.

Then Humphrey did something that no whale had ever done. Instead of swimming back out to sea, he went the wrong way up the Sacramento River.

The big river became smaller and smaller as
Humphrey traveled upstream.

He was looking for the ocean, but it was clear
Humphrey was lost.

Hundreds of people came to see Humphrey in the river. They would stare out at the water, waiting for him to come up for air. Then with a big whoosh his giant back would appear. And someone would shout, "There he is!" He was an amazing sight.

But something was wrong. Whales are supposed to live in the salt water of the ocean, not in the fresh water of rivers. A whale would die if it stayed in fresh water too long.

Humphrey was in trouble.

Everyone knew that Humphrey had to be turned back toward the ocean, but no one knew how to do that. After all, something like this had never happened before.

The farther Humphrey went the more worried everyone became...they wondered whether he was getting anything to eat...whether he was getting sick...or whether he would

beach himself in the river. One day, Humphrey squeezed
under a tiny bridge. It was so small no one could understand
how he had done it. Now he was really in trouble. He was
trapped.

The river beyond the bridge was very shallow and narrow.
It was so small Humphrey could hardly turn around. There
he was, a whale, stuck in a tiny stream, right in the middle of
a farmfield. It was hard to believe.

Something had to be done to get him out of there fast. Humphrey looked sick. The scientists knew he would die if he didn't get back to the ocean. Time was running out.

The people trying to save Humphrey would have to move fast. The scientists, Coast Guard officers and many others got together to work out a plan to save him. They decided to bang long pipes together underwater and scare him back down the river.

At the same time, they would play a recording that would broadcast underwater the sounds of whales eating. Maybe Humphrey would be so hungry and lonely he would swim toward the sound.

It worked! Humphrey turned around and started swimming back down the river. Everyone was relieved...but the danger wasn't over yet!

When Humphrey arrived at the little bridge, he stopped. He was afraid to go under it. He couldn't find a space big enough to go through.

People kept banging the pipes. Humphrey seemed flustered. What would he do?

As the pipes kept clanging, Humphrey became angry! He rolled from side to side and thrashed his great tail. People stopped banging the pipes.

But Humphrey's friends wouldn't give up. They knew they had to get him past the little bridge. If they didn't, he would die in the river.

The people trying to save him decided to make the space under the bridge bigger. They brought in a huge crane and worked through the night to clear away some of the old pilings.

Would Humphrey notice the difference?

The next day, the people began banging the pipes together again. Clang! Clang! The boats moved closer to Humphrey to urge him on toward the bridge.

This was his last chance. Everyone watched nervously.

Humphrey bravely approached the bridge. But as he tried to swim under it, his head became lodged between the pilings. He frantically bobbed his head up and down and thrashed his tail to free himself.

It was a terrible moment. The people trying to save Humphrey thought it might be the end. Humphrey was stuck.

Suddenly, Humphrey lifted one fin way out of the water, almost touching the bridge. As he twisted his body, he broke free from the pilings and swam through to the other side.

There was a shout from the banks of the river. Then another, and another, until everyone was cheering. "Hooray for Humphrey!" they shouted. He made it! Humphrey the lost whale was finally on his way home.

A whole flotilla of boats and the clanging of pipes behind
him helped Humphrey find his way down the river.
Finally, Humphrey arrived at San Francisco Bay.

Humphrey spent one whole day happily swimming around the Bay. He did tricks for the people gathered along the shore to see him one last time. They oohed when he slapped his tail. They aahed when he leaped into the air and belly flopped back into the water.

Humphrey seemed to be saying good-bye and thank you
to all his friends who had helped save his life.

The people who had helped rescue Humphrey also felt grateful. Humphrey had taught them a lot about humpback whales. He had also become a good friend. Many times during his ordeal, Humphrey could have simply flicked his tail and overturned boats carrying the people who were trying to help him. But he never did. He seemed to understand that they were his friends.

Finally, in the late afternoon fog, Humphrey swam under the Golden Gate Bridge and back out to sea.

Humphrey the whale had made it. He was finally home.

NOTES ABOUT HUMPHREY

Humphrey the Humpback Whale entered San Francisco Bay for the first time on October 10, 1985. For 26 days, this 45-foot-long, 40-ton giant captured the hearts of people everywhere as he tried to find his way back to the Pacific Ocean.

After Humphrey was rescued in 1985, he continued to visit the Bay Area during his annual migrations. He was spotted near the Farallon Islands in 1986 and again inside Bodega Bay in 1988. Scientists were able to identify him by the distinctive markings on his dorsal fin and tail flukes.

Then, early on the morning of October 22, 1990, people noticed a humpback whale beached on the mud in the shallow waters near Candlestick Park in San Francisco Bay. Later that day, scientists confirmed that it was our old friend Humphrey in trouble again.

For three days, rescuers from the Marine Mammal Center and the U.S. Coast Guard tried to free Humphrey from the mud. Finally, on the second day, they pumped air under him at high tide and towed him into deeper waters. Humphrey swam around San Francisco Bay for one more day before heading out to the Pacific Ocean under the Golden Gate Bridge . . . free, once again.

BILL PERRY

Humphrey has not been seen since 1991, when he was spotted near the Farallon Islands. But in May 2007 Humphrey's story was brought to mind when two humpback whales, a mother and her calf nicknamed Delta and Dawn, swam into San Francisco Bay for an extended visit. Delta and Dawn traveled about 20 miles farther inland than Humphrey did, way up the Sacramento River, where they stayed for days, seemingly trapped.

BILL PERRY

Veterinarians were worried since both whales had bad wounds that were getting infected. But after receiving antibiotics, Delta and Dawn improved and, thanks again to the efforts of many people and organizations, finally made their way out to the open waters of the Pacific.

Like Humphrey the Humpback Whale, Delta and Dawn had spent almost a month away from their natural habitat, making many friends and creating new interest in the lives of these magnificent marine mammals.

DARRYL BUSH/MWAUSA

Photos provided by the Marine Mammal Center, Sausalito, California, which headed up the efforts to rescue Humphrey in 1985 and 1990.

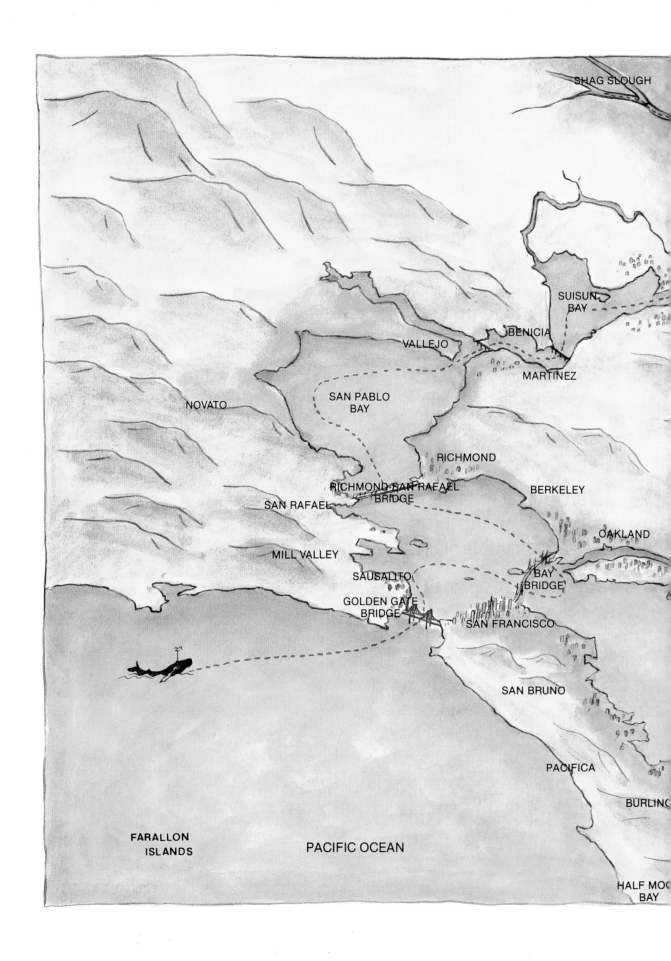